EXCEPTIONAL
AFRICAN AMERICANS

BEYONCÉ

*Singer, Songwriter,
and Actress*

Joseph Kampff

Enslow Publishing
101 W. 23rd Street
Suite 240
New York, NY 10011
USA
enslow.com

Words to Know

betray—To turn against or be unfaithful to someone.

charts—Lists that show the popularity of a song or an album.

depressed—Feeling deeply sad or discouraged.

destiny—What somebody will do or be in the future.

endorsement—A business agreement in which a famous person gets paid to say that he or she uses or likes a product.

feminist—A person who fights for women's rights and equality.

standing ovation—When the audience stands up and claps for a long time after a performance.

sue—To take someone to court and demand that he or she pay money for doing something wrong.

trio—A musical group with three people.

Contents

Beyoncé

CHAPTER 1

Destiny's Child

"Destiny" seems to perfectly describe Beyoncé Knowles's rise to stardom. When she was a little girl, Beyoncé's musical gifts were obvious to anyone who heard her perform. When Beyoncé was seven years old, she sang John Lennon's song "Imagine" at her school talent show. She received her first **standing ovation**. From this moment on, Beyoncé appeared to be destined for fame. But it was not easy. Beyoncé worked hard to be successful.

Beyoncé was born on September 4, 1981, in Houston, Texas. Her sister Solange was born in 1986.

Beyoncé's parents, Matthew and Tina, encouraged her to follow her dreams. Matthew quit his job so he could focus on helping his daughters succeed. He managed Girl's Tyme and Destiny's Child.

Beyoncé's parents, Matthew and Tina Knowles, made good livings and the family lived in a wealthy neighborhood in Houston. The girls went to Catholic school, and Beyoncé took ballet and jazz dance lessons. She also took vocal lessons and learned how to sing opera. Beyoncé was very shy when she was young. Singing and dancing helped her become more outgoing.

Early Music

Beyoncé was eight years old when she joined her first musical group, Girl's Tyme. Girl's Tyme got their first big break in 1992. They competed on the TV show *Star Search*. Beyoncé was heartbroken when they didn't win. "We were devastated, we thought our lives were over," Beyoncé explains. "But then again, that was my first time I lost something that I really wanted to win."

Beyoncé Says:

"Whenever I'm confused about something I ask God to reveal the answers to my questions, and he does. That's how we found our name—we opened up the Bible, and the word 'destiny' was right there."

The original members of Destiny's Child were, from left to right: LeToya Luckett, Beyoncé, LaTavia Roberson, and Kelly Rowland.

Then Beyoncé formed Destiny's Child with three other girls from Girl's Tyme. Destiny's Child constantly practiced singing and dancing over the next few years. They called their practice sessions "boot camp." Their hard work paid off when they released their first album, *Destiny's Child*, in 1998. The album sold more than a million copies. It was an amazing start for the group.

CHAPTER 2

Fame

In 1999 Destiny's Child released their second album, *The Writing's on the Wall*. It was the smash hit Beyoncé was hoping for. It sold more than nine million copies. And the hit singles "Bills, Bills, Bills" and "Say My Name" made the group famous all over the world.

But fame wasn't easy for Beyoncé. Touring all the time was hard work and the group was under a lot of pressure. Two of the original members of Destiny's Child didn't want Matthew Knowles to manage the group anymore. After they were fired

Destiny's Child hit it big with their second album in 1999. They began playing to much larger audiences.

from the group they said that Matthew treated them unfairly and they **sued** him.

This was a hard time for Beyoncé. She'd been through a lot with these women and she felt **betrayed**. Beyoncé says, "That's when I decided I only have two choices: I can be **depressed** and give up, or I can be positive and go on."

Moving On

Being positive worked out well for Beyoncé. Destiny's Child regrouped as a **trio** and released their third album, *Survivor*, in 2001. *Survivor* was Destiny's Child's most successful album yet. It went to the top of the **charts**. And the hit single "Survivor" won the Grammy Award for Best R&B Performance.

Beyoncé Says:

"I sometimes wish I could be anonymous walking down the street like everyone else. . . . . When you're famous, no one looks at you as a human anymore. You become property of the public."

Being famous can be tough. All of the members of the group wanted to take a break from Destiny's Child. After taking three years off, Destiny's Child reformed to release their last album, *Destiny Fulfilled*, in 2004. The group broke up the next year.

CHAPTER 3

New Directions

When Destiny's Child stopped performing, Beyoncé took her career in new directions. Beyoncé is not only a very talented singer; she's also a good actress. In 2001 Beyoncé started her movie career by starring alongside Mike Myers in *Austin Powers in Goldmember*. She played the role of Foxxy Cleopatra. Austin Powers was Beyoncé's breakout role on the big screen.

Beyoncé has acted in other movies, including *The Pink Panther*, *Dreamgirls*, and *Epic*. At first, Beyoncé was nervous about acting. She didn't want people to

Beyoncé and her *Dreamgirls* co-stars, Jennifer Hudson (far left) and Anike Noni Rose. The award-winning film allowed Beyoncé to use both her singing and acting skills.

think she only got acting jobs because she was a famous singer. She wanted to prove that she really could act. "I took a risk with acting," Beyoncé says. "It was scary because it was different for me. You just always have to take risks. I always go with my gut, and it's always right."

Pepsi and Perfume

Beyoncé became so famous that she was able to make many **endorsement** deals. She made a commercial for Pepsi with Britney Spears, Pink, and Enrique Iglesias. She has also endorsed perfumes, and even released her own very popular perfume line. Beyoncé started a fashion company with her mother called House of Deréon.

Beyoncé Says:

"My fans kept asking where they could get clothes like Destiny's Child's, so it was only natural for us to do a clothing line . . . I wanted to make sure it was true and honest and really something that we designed."

Beyoncé walks hand in hand with her mother, Tina, at a fashion show. The two started a successful clothing collection called House of Deréon.

CHAPTER 4

An Independent Woman

Beyoncé has done a lot of things in her life, but music has always been her main focus. Since Destiny's Child broke up, she has had a very successful solo career. Beyoncé's first solo album was *Dangerously in Love*. The biggest hit from the album was "Crazy in Love." She recorded the song with the famous rapper Jay Z (his real name is Shawn Carter).

A Full Life

A lot of people thought Beyoncé and Jay Z were dating. Beyoncé and Jay Z wanted to keep their personal lives out of the media. They kept their relationship secret until after they were married in 2008. In 2012 they had a baby girl named Blue Ivy Carter. Beyoncé says, "One thing that's for sure: The love that I have for music, for my husband, for my child, is something that will last far beyond my life."

Beyoncé released four other solo albums: *B'Day, I am… Sasha Fierce, 4,* and *Beyoncé*. She recorded

Beyoncé reunited with other members of Destiny's Child to perform at an awards show in 2015.

Beyoncé's husband, Jay Z, and daughter, Blue Ivy, join her onstage at the 2014 MTV Video Music Awards show.

To date, Beyoncé has won twenty Grammy Awards. She has been nominated for the award 53 times—more than any other woman in Grammy history.

her most recent album, *Beyoncé*, in secret. It was a surprise when it came out in 2013. The album explores many **feminist** themes. One of the issues she deals with is the pressure women feel to be beautiful.

Beyoncé is one of the most successful women in show business. She may really be "destiny's" child. But there is no doubt that she has always worked hard to make her vision come true.

Beyoncé Says:

"I always considered myself a feminist . . . It's just a person that believes in equality for men and women."

Timeline

1981—Beyoncé Giselle Knowles is born in Houston, Texas, on September 4.

1992—Beyoncé appears on *Star Search* with Girl's Tyme.

1998—Destiny's Child releases first album, *Destiny's Child*.

2001—Co-stars with Mike Myers in *Austin Powers* in *Goldmember*.

2003—Beyoncé releases her first solo album, *Dangerously in Love*.

2004—Destiny's Child releases their final album, *Destiny Fulfilled*.

2008—Beyoncé and Jay Z are married.

2012—Beyoncé and Jay Z have a baby girl named Blue Ivy Carter.

2013—Beyoncé releases the album *Beyoncé*.

Learn More

Books

Gagne, Tammy. *Day by Day With Beyoncé*. Hockessin, DE: Mitchell Lane: 2015.

Hill, Z. B. *Beyoncé*. Broomall, PA.: Mason Crest Publishers, 2012.

Susienka, Alexander. *Beyoncé*. New York: Cavendish Square Publishing, 2015.

Websites

beyoncé.com
Provides information about Beyoncé's music, fragrance line, tours, and media.

biography.com/people/beyonce-knowles-39230
Includes quick facts, a photo gallery, and quotations from Beyoncé.

Index

Published in 2016 by Enslow Publishing, LLC.
101 W. 23rd Street, Suite 240, New York, NY 10011

Copyright © 2016 by Enslow Publishing, LLC.
All rights reserved.

No part of this book may be reproduced by any means without
the written permission of the publisher.

Library of Congress Cataloging-in-Publication Data
Kampff, Joseph.
  Beyoncé : singer, songwriter, and actress / Joseph Kampff.
    pages cm. — (Exceptional African Americans)
  Includes bibliographical references and index.
  ISBN 978-0-7660-7170-4 (library binding)
  ISBN 978-0-7660-7178-0 (pbk.)
  ISBN 978-0-7660-7169-8 (6-pack)
  1. Beyoncé, 1981—Juvenile literature. 2. Singers—United
States—Biography—Juvenile literature. I. Title.
  ML3930.K66K36 2016
  782.42164092—dc23
  [B]
                      2015026937

Printed in the United States of America

To Our Readers: We have done our best to make sure all
website addresses in this book were active and appropriate
when we went to press. However, the author and the publisher
have no control over and assume no liability for the material
available on those websites or on any websites they may link
to. Any comments or suggestions can be sent by e-mail to
customerservice@enslow.com.

Photo Credits: Throughout book, © Toria/Shutterstock.com
(blue background); cover, pp. 1 Everett Collection/Shutterstock.
com; pp. 5, 16, 20 © AP Images; p. 6 Dave Hogan/Getty Images
Entertainment/Getty Images; p. 8 Jeff Kraviz/FilmMagic/Getty
Images; p. 10 Tim Mosenfelder/Getty Images Entertainment/
Getty Images; p. 12 Pam Francis/Hulton Archive/Getty Images;
p. 14 Bruce Gilkas/FilmMagic/Getty Images; p. 18 Erik Umphery
for Parkwood Entertainment/Getty Images Entertainment/Getty
Images; p. 19 Jason LcVeris/FilmMagic/Getty Images.